D0067844

In These Black Hands

By
Salisa Lynne Grant

For Myles

"I am a black woman
the music of my song
some sweet arpeggio of tears
is written in a minor key
and I
can be heard humming in the night
Can be heard
          humming
in the night"

—Mari Evans

Acknowledgements

This collection is dedicated to my son Myles. He was and is my greatest creation. His life and loss have propelled me to keep the promises that I made to him as well as the promises that I have made to myself. This collection is one of those promises. To the people who raised me, my mother Denise, my sister Lucreshia, and my brother De'Lon, "thank you" could never capture what you have done. I am undeniably and willingly yours. I love you with intention. For molding me, for your laughter, for loving me on purpose, I am infinitely grateful. Thank you to my friends who have called me poet when I forgot myself, and called me family when I needed it. To the people who hold me up when the weight of grief has caused me to collapse: Fatima, Shirkira, Nina, Michael, Allison, and Kendra. Thank you for seeing me and not looking away. Thank you to my colleagues and professors at Howard University. Your care and challenges have forced me to grow in ways that I did not know to be possible. To Evan: thank you for loving me and for loving our son. You have carried me to the end of this world and back. This project would only be a dream if it were not for my incredible publisher Janette Grant who also happens to be my cousin. Our family is vast, we are spread across many miles, but Janette's personal and professional support has been a light that will not dim. These people are proof of God's love for me. The ability to know God's love is the essence of a blessed life. I am so blessed. Lastly, to my people, Black lovers everywhere who smile in the face of fire. Thank you for teaching me what Black love is and what it can be.

Table of Contents

Part I
she called in her soul

Passing it On	1
she has always been all teeth	3
In These Black Hands	4
Fast	5
Providences	7
nebula	8
323	10
Covered	12
In the Night *for Stokely Carmichael/Kwame Ture*	13
Dreams for Sister	15
a too white moon	17
Wrestling Our Symphonies	18
Tenderheaded	23
three feet	25
Open Promise	27
she called in her soul	28

Part II
Black Lovings

Myles II	31
Storage	32
Equilibrium	34
quiet story *for Gene*	35

Five Little Girls *for Black Girls who cry in the Night*   37

Make Believe   39

We Let Wonder Take Us   41

Before you stop loving   43

My People   44

Myles III/Still Black   45

Pull   46

Brown boy   47

Night Surrounds Us   48

We On   49

An Answered Prayer   51

Instead We Roam   52

Black Lovings   53

Sunflower Monday   55

How dare we laugh?   56

Together   57

4 Hours in a Missouri Street *for Michael Brown*   58

Untitled   59

Her Body, a Museum   62

About the Author

Part I

she called in her soul

"*Here was peace. She pulled in her horizon like a great fish-net. Pulled it from around the waist of the world and draped it over her shoulder. So much of life in its meshes! She called in her soul to come and see.*"

—Zora Neale Hurston

Passing it On

She asked him,

"Where do the stars go in
the morning?"

And when he told her
they go inside of us,
she believed him.

Hugged herself tightly
and shined a blinding
smile in his direction.

"I can feel them in my fingers, my belly and
my nose."
He nodded and pointed
upwards, then at her.

"We carry them within us, and when
we smile, they show."

One day she will tell her children of their mother
who was born to laugh.

Stories will pass her tongue,
dancing on electric energy,

lips permanently formed into a stirring smile.

She will tell them of the times
she ran for her life, the purple nights that
turned violent, bodies dissolving, liquor that burned her chest and
made her brave. The times she was a stranger to fear.

Of the love, premature and premarital,
the love and reckless smoke that clouded her breath.

Of the times she imagined death, forgetting
its cousins-- hope, possibility, and future.

She will tell them of the fragmented bodies
she put back together, hearts and hands
egos and friendships, the
lives she saved, the trouble she caused and shared.

She might also tell them of the men who ran her wild
and made her crazy. The ones she refused to love,
and those who could never love her back.

She might, she will not remember everything,
but what she does, she will make theirs.

she has always been all teeth

she was taught to blend in early.
little girl with a colossal heart, beating
everybody's drums. her smiles
slowly became forced.

"smile young lady, lemme see those teeth."

eyes became weary. they stopped
dancing. instead they waited, they
were quiet. they fell soundlessly into
the shallowest pool. salty baby
girl blues.

she became
sorry by default. apologies in every
curl, her sense of touch grew
dull. growth, stunted.
she died and came back to haunt
her mother's memories.

i remember the moment i decided i wasn't
God. do you?

In These Black Hands

I would wake up in a small pool of velvet
wet
red
quickly drying
no pain, just damp,
just me, running across a clorox white pillow case
another pretty white thing ruined

a flutter of fear enters as I remember my mother's fury

I can't afford to buy new pillow cases every week little girl

but the butterflies settle as I remember hands
strong, sure, and brown
pushing my five year old head back to slow the
bleeding
her hands
running through a fresh relaxer

there is no hardness in these black hands
there is no anger in her hands
there is only love, there is only me

they tell the story her mouth will not allow.

Where does the red come from?

Fast

When your body betrays you
and the sun takes interest
in your lilac skin.

Guiding big men's eyes that
scratch through baby fat
leaving scars that
resemble grown
women.

No sweater thick enough.

Body bounces with each footfall. Each
stare, more painful
than the last.

Pupils cut like whiplash.

Her mind, acres away.
They
They catch every caterpillar stutter step, every butterfly sway.

They
They cannot help but call
her woman
call her fast.

They cannot help but call
her grown.

Every name except
her own.

Providences

surrounded, protected
water on all three sides
three coasts three
faces
shattered in laughter.

oceans in their own rights
bubbling beneath
choking death back
dancing into distance
they cannot escape.

mere tributaries, dependent on a temperamental
tide
land and sea converge where fault
lines, make threats as they fade
they are not pulled under, not
buried beneath an unforgiving beach
they are bruised, but breathing

submerged only in themselves, each other.

nebula

god placed one thousand galaxies between your two front teeth,
breathe,
exhale and ignite this city.
you,
are a living memory of play fights and fleeting moonlight.
of journeys north, then south
as each fluorescent footfall fostered flowers,
filled forests.
here, unwrap
a sandbox world, unprepared for your size,
for your dimpled brown thighs
your pull
with the sunrise.
smile,
and spray a love written in permanence across three counties.
dance,
raising clammy hands,
mahogany body spilling divine from distressed shorts and tops
you cropped.
body yours, yours, yours
sweat yours
voice yours
name yours.
you,
a euphoric fog
a real black night sky.
you,

too much for small petty places
you,
hard to pronounce
etched lightly into door jambs and handles
when and where you enter.

you,
making them work, for your gaze.
you,
galaxy girl
you,
crochet braids swinging
you,
muddy middle fingers at the ready.
you, a firestorm of laughter,
you are the now, the then, the hereafter.

323

A yellow miracle made from
paint, glass, and plaster.

Home for seven years or so.

We moved every year before
and every year after.

The walls had the chance to
turn beige with stories, the
floors creaked with puberty, prayers, and
patience.

We grew out of our bedrooms,
legs wouldn't fit any
longer.
Carpet knew too much and
backdoor was always slamming.

Telling the neighborhood our
best secrets.

In-home laundry room, built-in
spice racks.
A place to rest withered backs.

Even a hill for sledding.

Even a hill for sledding.

Covered

The floor sags under the weight.
One hundred years of memories
tied to my waist.
Forces me down, demands my
attention, compliance.
There is no point in resisting the pull.
Eyes forced open, mind override.
I cannot escape my grandfather's
grimace, my great grandmother's worry is worn around my neck,
I can still hear, the ring of my aunties' laughter.
Swimming in it, legs swinging, heavy with
knowing.
Each time I try to give up, to
submerge myself in ourtheir past,
theirmy arms push me upthrough.

There will be no drowning today.
Ok.

I will float on. Watching my body
disappear
reappear.

Covered in their lives.

In the Night
for Stokely Carmichael/Kwame Ture

You are the sweetest darkness.
A sweeping glow of sugar barely
kissing reality.

I cannot see you in the night
but I hear your wings as they
cry for release.

You are seven broken
waters, two fallen angels feathers bent,
one wrist that no longer bleeds.

You are a forgotten heart
beat, fighting to be heard over the
screaming, crying of life's let downs.

You speak, letting us know that we are still here,
you take our lips in your palm
and massage our every syllable.

You give us back the words that
set us, free, you
love us on principle, no charge no cost.

No receipt.

With all the chest of a King and the
fire of a Knight, you.
You, man of no armor no fear,
you, endless syllable of love

and
insistence,

You are the only poem
that makes us sing.

Sing sing sing.

Dreams for Sister

Last night I dreamt
of your engagement.
Of a love for you so powerful,
it swept you and
your pain away for awhile.
Surrounded you
and pulled you close.

Every smile you have
ever longed for
floated to your face.

A thousand gentle stares
were placed in
your palms.

In that moment you
were free.
You did not need
to be strong, no
one snatched the luminescence from within
you.

I stood back but near, where
only you could see me. Where only your light
would reach.

I waited, until your moment paused and
you began to look for me.

I waited, until you were ready to
share it.

I did my best.

Your eyes found mine
and there was only an avalanche of love.

Only friendship.
Only the indigo rhapsody of
our childhood.
Sisters who God fastened firmly
to one another.

For better or for worse.

I awoke, alive and ablaze.
Plotting for your joy.

a too white moon

That sounds so divine.
Your eyes on me,
soft.
Hands too, eventually.
The smell of you resting in
my nose.
Pretend forever, we are pretending
forever.
Your pretty smile, a too white
moon against a dark sky. I am
ticking. Like my mother showed
me how to do.
Ready to bury you in my
rubble.
I am not angry.
There is no fire here.
When I explode,
you'll know it.

I could never be divine, I am
all flesh and muscle, I am
nobody's God but
I know how to grow.
I can sit still and braid an
army, a movement, a nation.

Wrestling Our Symphonies

I.

Tonight there is no one
but
the memory of your shoulders,
broad as the base of Mt. Hood
strong as the spirits that forced me west.

I remember your song, it still rings in my bones,
moves between me in damp Oregon evenings.
How many nights did we mix spirits without blending bodies?—
I remember the sweetness of your sorrow.
Your smells of patience and forgiveness
still linger in my laughter.

Your steadiness is here too,
in the way I twist my hair.

In the morning, a puff of new blue sonnets
I release from my bonnet.

But tonight a wildfire brights me.
But does she fill your middle with wildflowers? send.

II.

I (cannot) love you.

I learned this in the
fourth grade when Todd called
me ugly after another kid accused him of liking
me. *She's BLACK. No.*

No.

Todd's cry baby ass actually did like me but would
never let anyone know it

(I will never let anyone know it)

I wanted to cry then
but
when
you look like we do.
Crying is off limits too.

I love you still.

III.

Love is the way I felt when I knew you were waiting for me.

I would quicken my already rapid pace or linger a little
longer as I crossed Snelling.
Fighting to remain neutral as
I pressed into the door. Opening
myself and leaving
it there for you
to sift through.

I waited for you too. I corrected your English
and imagined the arguments we would have.

You forgot to take the garbage out again.
You take up too much space in brown spaces.
Why can't I post pictures of us together online?

I always wanted to touch you, but there was rarely an excuse.

I remember that day in the French Quarter when you reached out
and
touched my arm, gently, like you wanted to feel how brown skin
felt in the sun.

I hope that is not why.

IV.

Maybe it was selfish
to leave you and come back.
Making you love me in polaroids,
flashes and smiles
wet with temporary.

I filled photo albums
wrestling our symphonies from old SD cards
and flash drives.

In our distance we allowed ourselves long drags and
tall glasses of "I miss you more."

What blanched me was learning that this is not just a thing people
say.
I actually missed you more. Made you love me
and put myself firmly in the middle of you.

Not knowing your goodbyes had already been signed and sent.
My reply was a chalice of sour tears, spoiled.

My eyes may never dry fully.

V.

My love for you lit up downtown
Portland tonight, as I crossed the Burnside

Bridge on foot and on the phone.
I knew
that somewhere, everywhere you were
sitting with a packed heart and
a stirring mind. I knew that you
were full of me and
the volume of my love.

I was instantly in love and sorry.

Sorry because my love can have the tendency to break and there is
no doubt that you have begun to
splinter.

I do not want to know how to
turn down the July of my passion
but I hope
I hope you never long
for an early winter.

I watched the lights grow stronger
sprinkled against the blue brown backdrop.
Attempted
to locate you in the stars.
We could always find each other
in the thickest rooms.

Tenderheaded

Come sit here now
beneath the mahogany mountain that is me.
Bring the fluffy pillow from
your bed.
Grab the hard bristle brush and hair
grease.

Sit still as I weave these mazes and maps little girl, I don't
have all night.
Lord, I never knew a more
tenderheaded child in all my damn life.

Girl you better stop twistin n turnin n
lean your
head this way. Follow the rough curves of my hands.
Let heavy fingers paint history
in every dainty hair strand.

Yes, you almost done. Tsk.
You'd think it was torture.

Look at my pretty baby, go get
the mirror in the corner.

See what we made.

Me and God did somethin

special
on your birthday.

three feet

wooden beds bunked and mismatched
pillow cases.
the sound of brown bottles
singing beneath,
our laughter
its own echo.

we dreamed together, i am
sure of it.
our stories carried us off into
the night. there was
safety there, there was no
fire, no listening for keys in

front doors.
we were each other's medium
brown havens.

full of questions and never
hindered by answers.
full of rich fairy tales and
soft journeys away from a hard home.

full of pink promise and
purple barrettes.

i could hear every movement

you made in your sleep.
every twist of your body,
every shake of your beads.

a resting rainbow below me.
parted by three feet.

Open Promise

I promise that when you forget how to smile,
I will remind you
I will place
two field hands onto
the earth of your face
and position your glowing African lips into
a crescent moon not unlike the one that
followed our true founding mothers and fathers to freedom.

I will shake away the thick coat of dust and ash
of deceit, desperation, and lies
that threatens to bury us all alive
I will fight heart to heaven combat with each painful memory
every nightmare, fear, and flash.

I will do all of this

I will carry your spirit on my shoulders,
and write sonnets to your self esteem,
walk barefoot and open souled to my death with no hesitation,
and cry out freedom songs to your dreams.

I will do all of this

Only asking for one gesture in return,
that you do the same for me.

she called in her soul

when the street lights came on
she worked through knotted hands
and shortness of breath
doing all she knew to do
all she'd ever known
she survived
she practiced surviving on nothing
in preparation for the day
the Big White Man who thought
he lived in the sky and her
bedroom and her heart
would come to take it from her
they always did
they always took things from women like
her
when the hour got late she'd
pretend she was with Jesus
trying to remember what
her mother had tried to teach
her
she'd try to believe
she'd put on her best
front-pew sinner face
we were all with him before
we breathed life
she pulled together all the faith
her mother had left in the cupboards

and gathered it under her
pillow no matter how
withered splintered broken
it may be
as the day ended she lifted
her light from its place
between her breasts and blew
it out for safe keeping
tomorrow
she'd try her best to get it lit again

Part II

Black Lovings

"Yes, we were trembling. We have not stopped trembling yet, but if we had not loved each other, none of us would have survived..." —James Baldwin

Myles II

The sunrise touched you
but it did not take you
away.
The sunrise touched you
and I cried into myself.
You felt no pain.
You only felt me.
The sunrise touched you.
It did not warm but
it caressed. I wanted you
to feel it, to see it.
I wanted you back.

The moon held on tight.
You belonged to me, to
her, to the night.
My skin still trembles from
missing.

"How is it possible, how is it
that such a pretty day
can cause so much pain?"

I want to scream at every moon.
Give me my sun back.

Storage

watching the sunrise
from the pool deck
still damp with yesterday's rains.
all 27 years of you. all ten thousand tears,
every lightyear of laughter.
the chill of the heavy morning, where the breeze tickled your
arms
and the birds crooned hello.
loving who you loved. still,
endlessly, divorced from logic.

the questions
that pushed you forward, and the ones that paused you.
asking yourself how you got here, why the days seem to drag
on in solitude, when will you find your own testimony?
the inertia, the deadlocks, and the uprisings
that burned inside you.
the insomnia, the wine, Jeff Buckley's tenor, and
all the ways
your body resisted.
the ways your body carried the moon,
wore it under polka dot overall shorts and floral head wraps.

remember it all and if you cannot,
remember
tell someone what you saw,
what you

knew. let them,
remember for you.

Equilibrium

swinging, billie style
watch, the swoon and swell.
bodies, blessed with violence
here, marvel at our bullet casing bracelets
watch, us froth and frolic
tongues, dangling with luxury.

quiet story
for Gene

we sat together
loving him and
scared, we felt campus housing carpet
scratch the soles of our feet.

we would not let him disappear.
tired, we watched headlines and stared and stared
and saw, one of ours taken. saw us unimagined,
watched as sparkler gave in to wind.
he was,
gone from us.

no more Louisiana drawl
good mawnin,
no more
get ya hair lined up gul.

the evening was long with story, and with fear.
tears came, not in waves, there was no build.
they came like little bombs, planted in the corners of us,
came like concrete fists.

there was no howling only cold,
only questions and,
but he was the good one.

we stayed too quiet, lifting the moon with our nerves
sent email after email
to whom it may concern
we love him,
he is ours.

we loved him as we loved each other
one keystroke at a time.

Five Little Girls
for Black Girls who cry in the Night

i remember the day that i met her
this fifth little girl,
still too small, playing dress-up in her sister's clothes,
though not a girl any longer.

she was
there
there was another,

she laid
broken babied like the others
burning and blinded by shattered glass,
mind a jumble of fear.

she survived
to tell the story of the past
that no one wanted to hear.

she stood
skin too black like me, slight, slim, all arms and knees,
the shine of her skin shook me, glowing as if she were still aflame,
she told me her fears, gave me the gift of her pain, our pain, to
keep.
lit up by her words, i stuffed her soul in my purse,

watched her focus on every word

as she told a room of burning black women her story.

"We were victims of terrorism too,
1963 was no different from 2001. We have nothing, no one
wants to hear us."

that day i sat, 19 years old and exploding,
felt the skin around my eyes melt and drip away.
she could barely see me,
as the tears set fire to my face.

"I lost four friends that day, lost my best friend, lost my sister, lost
my faith."
the ashes tickled my withered eyelashes as I reached for her hand,
she shook all of me awake as I mumbled my blazing thanks,
wanting only to say:

I will survive, I will tell it too.
We are still losing our sisters to fires we cannot douse, today.

Make Believe

That the past can stay there
even though it is ever moving, swelling beneath us.
It creeps around on all fours
whispering our deepest fears into
frostbitten ears.
Do not listen. Fight the urge to
gallop backward into the frightening white
fog.
Keep the remembers at the bottom
of your shoe
wearing them out with each step
ahead. Do not allow them to rise.

Light your journey with manicured
memories and heavy pause.

The back of you will always be
there, as a reminder.
The body never shakes the
scared sweats completely.
Bend forward into the warm light, despite the
gray nightmares and missing
middle.

Leap out of the way of the
torment that turns your teeth to tinsel.

Come, frolic in the gaps.

We Let Wonder Take Us

If we are killed, let it be known
that we saw the mountains and
both oceans tickled our feet.

Let it be known that
we never let the fog or
our cloudy sunrises
keep us inward.
We shrugged off the rain
and stepped out of our doors.

We made a point to love the darkest
days. The ones that lingered like
smoke and cigarette burns in the
carpet.

Those nights were always our favorite.
We traded riches for thick-lipped
kisses and wonder.

We let the wonder take us.

Our love was our only captor
everything was movement and
wrong didn't mean anything to us.
Then.
We left reason in the back of our

mothers' closets and hoola-hooped
with inhibition and fright.

Let it be known that we died in
battle, bombs strapped to our hearts, loving us into existence
fighting for our people. Searching
for dreams delivered at the bottoms
of our father's vodka bottles and
rivers that killed.

Dying for the night. Dying for the right to live and to love
ourselves.

Before you stop loving

me I want you to
see.
All of the ways you will
be losing.
Fall down inside of my fingers
and become.
Find it inside of you.
Inside of you is the only you
I need.
Beautiful, quiet, unbearable, you.
I can see you fading.
Fading out in my light.
Blinded and held captive.
Captive in my own lost love.
Don't go missing. Please.
I see you but I think you
are getting ready.
Shoes on, back turned.
Pain left in forgotten slippers
underneath the bed.
Don't go until I'm ready not
to fall.
Fall down inside of myself.
I need this. One last thing.
Become.

My People

An assortment of
sweets and sours all lined
up
in order of interaction.

My people are stories.

Full of missing pieces and
laughs that dance.
Sometimes I read through
them and cry. I have
to catch myself before
my tears damage the
pages.

The pages feel like all
that I have sometimes.
I won't give up remembering
I won't give up.

My people.

Myles III/Still Black

Half of me swims beneath
your chest.
I hear my words enclosed in
your breath.
I am a moment
fleeting,
monumental, soul-grasping,
and sustaining.
You are the light that
streams through me.

What is the night without
the moon?
Still black, still endless, still
moving.
But it is without its pair,
its illuminating
love.

Pull

Steam raising from sun soaked
skin. What does it mean
to embody the moon and
mimic the sun?
Carrying yellows and golds
inside of you as you
chase after the night.
Following dusky stillness,
on fire with dawn's love.

You stay warm, you stay
lighting us all with
your memories.
We try to ignore the
pull. Taking us from
the now. Releasing us
in the past and leaving
us there to roam.

I am, we are still there
even as we work, play,
live. Trapped in you,
wet and warm with
remembers.

Brown boy

I am sorry you could not
stay. I wish the
world was ours and
that we could walk
together.
I will never stop dreaming
of your smile, your
open eyes and your
sunshine future.
Your life was brief but
you are a lifetime. You
are the best part of
me, of my life. You
brown boy that I love,
I cannot ever be
without you. I am
you. We are one
and the same.
The same yellow
sunrise. Bright and
fleeting.

Night Surrounds Us

Long evenings that
linger like scents
of rose.

Waiting. So many
minutes piled into
waiting. The moon
plays hide and seek
with the sun and
we run.

From memories, faces
sleepless nights and
fear.

Fear that mutes movement
and steals sound.

Long evenings that
sample songs of mourning.
A deep blue that settles
into the blackest black.

Night surrounds us and
we tuck away our smiles.

We On

This world was never ready for the
swell of you.
So let them wonder.
Let their pondering buzz around you like
the thirsty honey bees.
Move against their music, side-stepping
questions that never seem to
end. Just
wait.

We on the way.

Follow the crystal moonlight when you lose
your footing.
Do not fear the loss, the win, the
draw. Remember the feeling of resting
on cold concrete, the lines left in your legs,
the tear streaks you wore proudly for decades.
Hold on.

We on the way.

Create, blast, breathe beautiful into
the cold forsaken places.
Do not be afraid to cast
shadows, spells, memories that suffocate.

Fold my hands into yours and listen for the looming sunrise and remember.

We on our way.

An Answered Prayer

I prayed for you. I loved
you into life.
There were nights before you
when I kneaded my belly
making room for all of you.
Big smile.
A laugh that rocks a room.
The music of you.
I saw you coming.

In the corners of my dreams.
In my most vivid visions.
I was a witness. I am.
Then and now.
Even now. I watch you flit
and groove into spaces too small
for you.

And collapse whole worlds.
I sit, hands in my lap.
Sight not what it once was.
But I can see all of you.
Every single step.

Instead We Roam

The sunsets sing songs
of longing.
As the light fades we
let the insides out.

Our less flattering, painful
selves come creeping and
we turn to face the
moon.

We cannot hope to swim
among the stars tonight.
They close the doors in
our faces and prepare
their judgement.

Instead we roam and
play in the red dust.
We listen as the music
rises and swells.

Taking us with it.
Taking us away and
never promising a return.

We listen as the day dies.

Black Lovings

The kinds that seep deep
into
you like, like the night
air when the sun retreats.

The kinds that sing softly over
you while you travel through timeless
dreams.

The kinds that grip you by sunkissed
shoulders and shake awake
the universe that resides inside.

The kinds that not even death could stop.

It is the kind that wanders in and out of
spirits' worlds in search of redemption.

It is a mother in one cold place,
a warm son in another. A golden
line that keeps them tethered to each other.

The Black Lovings are concrete
ridges in the soles of our feet.

No longer for sale, we have always been
Free.

Black Lovings is baby's breath, Jamaican
rum, spitting laughter through fire
tears.

Black Lovings is
an untamable ocean,
murderous, and fierce.

Sunflower Monday

This, our yellow day, will be
centuries long. Petals
spread at your oak feet,
feel your hands sink into
the earth.

A beginning, a beginning, a
beginning.
Delicate, growing perfectly impermanent.

I walked the city streets in
ninety degree DC heat to meet you
and your love.
Found you tucked under

couch cushions and geometric
rugs.

Thank you for sour saturday
nights and crowded sundays.
Thank you most of all for our

Sunflower Monday.

How dare we laugh?

How dare we laugh in this
world they say is not ours to seek?
How dare we sit up, black
backs tall and strong against
our seats?

How dare we light flames in
small places? Blazing the confinement
offered. How dare we

Be.
Breathe.
See.

How dare we call ourselves, set
ourselves, make ourselves

Free.

Together

Weathered and warm
I rest in your cobalt shadow, there
is love here and, there is
home here.

Moonshine kisses on collar bone,
mixing melanin with mist.

You hold my
broken body
in your dry coral palms.

Put me together again.

Chipped here and there. No
worse for wear.

4 Hours in a Missouri Street
for Michael Brown

In the summertime,
in the summertime
our skin shines, glows like target
practice.

In the summertime,
in the summertime
our smiles sing, against ebony
skin, hard to swallow. Straight
gin.

In the summertime,
in the summertime our laughs
bounce off walls like tennis
balls. Unhidden.

In the summertime we glisten,
too bright for simple eyes.
In the summertime we do not die.
In the summertime we fly, rise.

Untitled

I have written you one million
songs. Lullabies and ballads
alike.

They all sound like the
breaths you will never
take. They all make
me moan from deep
within.

The moan of a childless mother
left clawing at her skin.

The pain is always moments
away, inches.
I refuse to pack it up
in boxes with the rest of you.

Instead I
let it rise as
it pleases. Lean towards the
hurricane, tip my hat
to typhoon.

Grasp it around the waist.

Embrace.

The pain is memory, it is confirmation that
you were here.
We were here. Together.
The fear, the love,
the way my body shook. I am
still shaking now.

You taught me to stop
performing. The show stopped
the day that you arrived.

No more time to pretend,
no more space to hide.
No more someone else's vibrato or
strangers' pirouettes.

I am lyricist, choreographer,
and director
now.

I run spotlight and sing
the big solo too.

The songs I wrote for you
are tattooed on the insides of my forearms.
They are there for
safekeeping. Here they
sit.

Alongside everything I
never told you.

In my arms where I
will not get to hold you.

I will sing them until the
world knows them word
for word.

Sing with me now.

Her Body, a Museum

She is a woman in repair.
Body aches and nightmares
skip, through her.

Each day,
a reminder of
what is not, what was, what
will not be.

Shoelaces bind her together as
she learns to walk again.
Learns to breathe again.
Learns to
be
again.

She is with the sun as it peeks behind
the doughy clouds.

Why is this place, this clear
and cloudy place the only
one she calls home?

Why does the red dirt under
fingernails, offer comfort? Her hair

dry, unlike sharp coal

eyes, unlike slippery
palms that leave gray sky stains.

Her mind, a bundle of impatient
fireworks.
Each one waiting its turn
to blow.

Her body, a museum.
Here, beauty has a home.

About the Author

Salisa Lynne Grant was born in Providence, Rhode Island and raised in Duluth, Minnesota. Her first love is and always will be poetry. Her second love is her son Myles who lives within her heart and within her art. For more from Salisa readers can find her work in the poetry anthology *Scattered Petals: poetry for remembering faith, hope, patience and courage* and the forthcoming poetry anthology *A Garden for Black Joy: Global Poetry from the Edges of Liberation and Living.* Readers can also find content from Salisa on her Youtube Channel: "Foreseeing Salisa" and her Instagram: @foreseeingsalisa. Salisa is completing her PhD in African American Literature at Howard University and works as an English professor. She currently resides in the Washington DC area.

Made in the USA
Monee, IL
06 January 2020